Heartfelt Prayers
of Thanks and Hope

Heartfelt Prayers
of Thanks *and* Hope

by JOHN H. GAROT

RESOURCE *Publications* • Eugene, Oregon

HEARTFELT PRAYERS OF THANKS AND HOPE

Resource Publications
An Imprint of Wipf and Stock Publishers
199 W. 8th Ave., Suite 3
Eugene, OR 97401

www.wipfandstock.com

PAPERBACK ISBN: 978-1-6667-3032-6
HARDCOVER ISBN: 978-1-6667-2167-6
EBOOK ISBN: 978-1-6667-2170-6

08/06/21

Contents

Thanks

About the Author

John H. Garot earned a BA degree at St. John's University in Collegeville, MN., and an MA degree at Arizona State University. Following, he joined the military for two years in the Vietnam era, and then taught secondary school. Later, Garot launched a career in industry with the Miller Brewing Company, the Outboard Marine Corporation, and Motorola and Motorola Cellular, specializing in advertising, sales promotion, and PR. In retirement, he returned to teaching at the college level, and is now an associate professor.

Childhood

Lord Jesus, Teach me How

I beg of thee to impart onto me,
The skills to share and the truth to see.
I pray daily for your grace and goodwill.
Pardon my sins and lead me where Thou will!
Help me as I make my way over ground and sea.
Until such time I'll be with Thee for all eternity.
Through Christ Jesus, our Lord and Savior! Amen.

My Pet Gift from the Lord

I was truly sad and lonely, filled with despair.

And across my path came a furry little fellow that looked like a bear.

He stopped in front of me, as if to say, "How are thee?"

I jumped for joy and knelt on one knee,

To pet him gently and show him how I care, over and over.

He rolled about, as if he were prancing in freshly cut clover.

Today, he is mine. Thanks to you, my Lord.

I will never forget to thank You, over and over, for the great reward!

Praise the Lord Jesus, my Master on high who gave us the sun,

the moon and the sky! Amen.

Through Your Loving Grace

God, I implore your loving grace to help me
Lead a spiritual life, helping others,
Sharing my talents and successes,
And being able to worship thee every day of my life!
I further implore you to shed your grace on me
To help me understand how to follow your will,
In making the right decisions in life . . .
And to let go of those problems and situations,
That only YOU can solve.
This, I ask through Your Son, Jesus Christ,
Our Lord and Savior. Amen!

To Trust in God

When I was young, I asked my Mom, who is this guy they all call
    God?
It sounded very strange and just a bit odd. . .
Here are her words of wisdom for all to share.
"He's in our hearts, our minds, our bodies and souls.
Wishing us well and keeping us on the trail of life.
Regardless of hardship, failure, or strife.
Whenever we need Him, He is always there,
Whether you are kneeling in prayer or sitting in a chair.
And while you sleep, He kindly protects you and your little teddy
    bear!"
Praise be the Lord Jesus on High! Without your protection and
    hope,
I'd never make it through the night, much less the day.

Despair

Dear God, I Need Your Help!

Dear God, I turn to Thee in time of need.
I have nowhere to turn, but to Thee.
My soul is in need. My body in turmoil.
There is nothing to reap; my soul is soiled!
Please forgive me for my many sins and fault.
I promise to change and amend my ways.
My life is short, indeed. Just a matter of days!
I beg for your forgiveness, every which way!
To Thee, I pray. . .To Thee, I pray!
Praise be God, our heavenly King. Now and Forever.
Amen.

Save Us from War

They came from the East, the West, the South and the North.
Looking for wealth, success, and growth.
But left behind death, ruin, and zero discourse!
When will we learn? To whom can we turn?
How many more lives must we lose before we learn?
Save us, oh Lord, before we are burned!
Blessed be the name of the Lord. Amen.

The Final Sigh

I look about the room and see smiles and joy, faith and hope.
But I'm nearing the very end of life on my final rope.
It was wonderful spending so much time with family and friends,
But the good Lord has called me home. My body no longer
bends!
The aches and pain have taken their toll on my heart and limbs.
I must soon leave. I love you all, from family to all my kin.
Bless the Lord Jesus, for he is kind and forgiving. I'll see you all
soon in the house of the Lord, called Heaven. Amen.

The Meaning of War

Lord, oh Lord, what have we done!
Two world wars with thousands buried in the sands of time. . .
When will we learn the 'real' enemy is neither in front or behind.
I beseech Thee to hear my plea . . .You who have given your life
for all mankind.
Open the door for final peace for the 'richest' to the 'least'.
Once and for all, silence the beast!
Through Jesus Christ, our King. Amen.

The Time Has Come, The Time has Come!

The time has come to lay our weapons down,
To stop the bombs and pounding of the ground.
The time has come to look homeward bound. . .
To rejoin our loved ones on our home ground.
Before my son or daughter die,
Let us confess to the lies.
Too many sisters and brothers have been lost,
Too many stormy nights have I, at the wailing wall, tossed.
Come home, one and all, and join hands with me,
We are waiting with open arms for thee. . .
Yet for many, it will be a homecoming never to be.
Come home before I get the folded flag on my lap, neatly lain,
She was a hero who died "not in vain".
Empty consolation for all our grief and pain.
In a land far away, she will forever remain!
God bless America and come home sane. Amen.

Education

Praise to the Lord on High

The cold winds blow, but they won't last.
The summer breezes will be back!
It is the Lord, I praise for that. . .
He brings me joy and saving grace.
Throughout my life, He has helped me win the race,
From step one to the final setting of the sun.
He has been with me in thought and prayer,
Never forgotten, yet always near!
Praise the Lord, Jesus, now and forever. Amen.

Teachers

Whether one or many, you have helped us all.
You have shaped our lives and helped us grow from little to tall!
From books to computers, you have taken our hands,
And explained the wisdom across the lands.
If understanding were a problem at times,
You would take a pause and redraw the lines.
We are who we are today because you never gave up or said 'No'.
"Try it again," you would say, "but maybe change your pace to
    slow, in order to
reach your goal."
Thank you, dear Lord, for all the wonderful teachers throughout
    the land,
Without whose help we would be unable to stand!

The Degree is in Sight!

What was once a dream, will soon be in my hand!
I can see it, I can feel it, I can hear my name, calling me to the
graduation stand.
Six long years have I toiled in the candlelight of the night,
Striving to learn, hoping to remember, dividing wrong from
right.
All that is left is one last exam, one last moment of anguish and
pain.
I hope I can endure, do well, and not go insane. . .
This is the moment. This is the time. This is the prize.
Dear Lord, I thank thee for all that You have done!
I shall sing Your praises on high, until my final day will come!

To Learn or Not to Learn

In the early grades an Instructor said, 'It's up to you to learn or
    not to learn!
I only present the material and help you to discern!'
Words of wisdom, indeed they were, and true-to-life as the rising
    sun.
It was with earnestness and dedication I approached school on
    the run.
I could not wait to learn more, Lord, about Thee, life, and
    eternity!
Each day before the final bell, we'd honor Thee with bent knees.
And at the end of each night, I will deeply thank Thee,
For all the help and good grace you've shared with me!
Praise the Lord Jesus. Amen.

The Bond of Marriage

That very special day and lifetime moment: I for thee, and thee
for me!

Throughout the years and tears, we gladly sang and lightly
pranced.

As if we were touched by the eternal lance!

Yet, as we age and live through one generation to the next, we'll
never

forget the day we were blessed!

Although the bones are not as strong as once they were, we are

committed to help one another until the final call and eternal
rest!

Praise to our Lord, Jesus Christ. Amen.

Faith

Church

A place of worship, a place of joy, a place to see Thee, face-to-face.

A time to rest, reflect, and thank Thee for your precious grace.

As I look upon the cross above, I see nothing but unlimited love,

For all of us creatures, offspring, and all You can view from far
above.

It was with kindness, understanding and hope,

You shed your life so that all mankind can continue to cope.

Thank you, dear Jesus, far above, for your eternal love and
support, In times of

stress and happiness, from port to port! Amen.

Firstborn, Stillborn

Dear Lord, you claimed a young saint in Heaven before she was
   born.
She didn't have a chance to come home. She left us totally alone.
She is resting now in quietness and peace, beneath a small
   headstone.
With sadness and tears, we said to her, 'Goodbye forevermore'.
And now we hope to see her when we finally reach Your door.
Take care of her and hold her close. She was a beauty to behold.
To us, she was far more than fame and fortune, or even gold!
Thank you, Lord Jesus, for what You've done to help us rise and
   see the setting sun.
When all is done, we shall see You then, and hold our firstborn in
   our arms again. Amen.

The Cross

Just a piece of wood with another going across,

Yet, you gave up your life, dear Jesus, so none of us would be lost.

It is with deepest thanks, I pray to Thee today,

For my personal thanks and the opportunity to join you in
Heaven one day.

Mankind's sins of evil and discord nailed you to the wood,

Yet, you forgave mankind, past and present, as well as you could.

20 centuries later we go to church to pray, to honor You wherein
you lay.

Your words still live and help us along the way, until one day, we
can beside they stay!

Lord Jesus, our many thanks to Thee, for carrying the remnants
of the tree!

We will greet you in Heaven, when we are free. Amen.

The Final Call

Lord, Oh Lord, bring me home.
When my time comes, leave me not alone.
I shall sing thy praises on high.
My voice shall reach beyond the sky!
It is 'I', Oh, Lord. I shall follow you,
To eternity and the forever blue.
When my life's over, it will begin anew,
In the arms of my Lord. I love you!
Save me, Oh Lord, save me!
Sprinkle your graces upon my brow,
I shall wait for Thee and the final call.
Lord, bring me home. I'm ready now.
Through Christ Jesus, our Lord. Amen.

Three in One

Father, Son, and Holy Ghost,
I love you all, but the Lord the most.
On the final day, I shall reach for your hand
And follow your footsteps in yesterday's sand.
Take my hand and lead me home. . .
I'm heaven bound and never alone.
Thank you, Lord, for the good life.
Filled with joy and lack of strife.
I'm thankful to you for all eternity,
                    For all eternity . . .
Blessed be the Trinity, Father, Son, and
Holy Ghost. Amen.

The Two of Us

Come, stand beside me, and we shall overcome,

Whatever evils or sadness we encounter before the setting of the
sun.

Together, as the sun rises in the morn, we will bury forever the
forlorn.

Very soon our gift from God will be born.

It is time to rejoice and praise the Lord,

'Though the finest and most precious we cannot afford.

Thank you, dear Lord, for all You have provided. We deeply
appreciate it,

And will get it equally divided. Amen.

Growing Up

Friends

Those who disagree should not be lost,
But rather heard and listened to,
Regardless of background or the mistakes of a few.
The truth they carry from beginning to end,
Should be heard as if they are all our friends.
For it is truth, honesty and honor that truly count,
in the very end.
Blessed be our Lord, Jesus Christ. Amen.

Goodnight Sunset

In my youth, I would look to the West and search for his smile,

As the sun would fall and say, "My day is done! I can stay but a
brief while."

I would thank him with deep sincerity and hope to see him rise
again.

So that we children can rise, and our daily games begin.

No matter how hard or fast I would run up the walk to give the
sun my final talk,

He would still slowly disappear and let the night take over the
walk.

"Oh, sun, oh, sun, when will I see you again? I hope it's soon, but
we must make

room for the moon."

Both make my happiness bloom, but I love the sun above all the
rest!

Praise the Lord, Jesus, for His wonderous gifts of day and night,
heat and light.

Amen.

Grandma

"Come here, my grandson, and let me wipe the tears,
Ahead of you lies happiness and many, many good years.
Obey your Mom, do your best in school, and you will find
success will forever be yours.
Whenever you need to talk or share your load, come see me, dear,
and I'll help you even more.
And when we part, think of me always standing by your side,
As the waters of life shift back and forth like the tide."
Thank you, Lord Jesus, for a wonderful and loving Grandma.
She's more than I've ever deserved, and she's back now with
Grandpa. Amen.

The Love of Pets

The good Lord gave us pets for a reason,
To help us get through each-and-every season!
Whether one is down and out, or overjoyed with delight,
A pet will stand close-by to share and console one's life.
The next time you see a pet, say a prayer that we
can all draw nearer and share!
Praise the Lord Jesus on high. Amen.

The Easter Hunt

"Where is my basket? Where is my candy? Inside or out?
    Upstairs or down?
I'll find it wherever it is and get it before the cat can turn around!"
This was the fun, the enjoyment, and the thrill of Easter Sunday.
No one told me it was a day set aside to give the Lord respect and
    high praise,
For all He had done for me and all mankind, leaving no one
    behind.
As the years passed, the reality set in and I began to praise Jesus,
    truly one of a kind!
Now, the candy is minimal and no longer a thrill, replaced by
    Church and following His will. . .
Thank you, Lord Jesus, for all you have done for all mankind
    under the sun.
Amen.

The Big Boom

It comes but once a year in early July,
Just when the notorious bugs begin to fly.
There are firecrackers galore, from shore to shore.
But never again will I ever get more!
I piled them up as high as I could,
And then started a fire as if they were wood.
Boom, crack, and whistling through the night,
They shot through the sky and illuminated it bright.
And taught me a lesson that I'll never take light.
Praise the Lord for safety that night and every night thereafter!
Amen.

Hope

Final Steps

Lord, your steps still stand in the sands of time.
The years have passed, but you are still mine.
I shall follow you one last time . . .
To eternity and rest.
When the final bell rings, I shall rise no less,
And honor Thee with the deepest prayer from my
humble breast!
I'm ready, Lord, to follow your steps.
Through Christ Jesus, our Lord. Amen

Hope

Is it a word, a faith, a way of life?
It can see us all through our pain, suffering and strife.
There may or may not be answers for all,
But we must continue in the positive lane and never stall.
The very best, oh Lord, to one and all!
Blessed be Father, Son, and Holy Ghost. Amen

Humility

Is it a gift or something divine? From the Lord or something I might find?

It would seem to come from on high. . .something the Lord may have left behind.

How much more can a man give than His life nailed to a tree?

I beseech Thee, oh Lord, on high, share your spirit and humility with me!

I try day-in and day-out to listen carefully to others and gain from their thoughts,

But often I feel I'm greater because of what I've been taught.

When reflecting on Thee, it is all forgot and my efforts are truly for naught.

With humility and courage, I can help others gain and truly respect Your divine name.

Thank you, oh Lord, thank you for Your wisdom and humble fame!

Oh, Lord, I've Met my Match

I've prayed my best to ask for help and hope.

My prayers went un-answered, and I continued downward on an
even slope!

It was then that I asked once again, more humbly, to learn how to
cope.

With Your good grace and kind words, my prayers relieved the
pain!

Through graciousness and goodness on high, my future is
moving upward once again.

I can take comfort this Fall season and refill my empty bin!

Thank you, Lord Jesus, and Mother too. Thank you on high.
You've made a grown man cry.

With My Lord, There's Always Hope!

My day is done, with little to show at the setting of the sun.
Yet my hopes are high, as I have another day soon to come!
With your help, oh Lord, I shall cling to hope tomorrow,
And tomorrow, and tomorrow.
There's no end in sight as you lead me along Your way.
I shall follow your steps and do as You always say!
Praise be the Lord Jesus. Today, tomorrow, and for eternity.
    Amen.

Wisdom

Oh Lord above, Majesty of Majesties, I implore Thee,

Grant me the wisdom it takes to learn, to apply, and finally to be free.

I've tried and I've tried, but my efforts have all fallen flat.

I still have the monkey on my back.

Through prayer and alms giving, I was assured of hope, peace, and eternal life.

But the only return in my short-lived life was the extension of my current strife!

Lord, relieve me of the bondage of self, and clothe me in heavenly wisdom,

So that I will be prepared to see Thee, face-to-face, as I enter the final Kingdom.

Amen.

Loneliness

Lord Jesus, Help me Overcome

My life is filled with fear and apprehension.
A decision, I cannot make, nor overcome depression.
With Thee at my side, I'm confident and sure.
My decisions will be right and my fear cured.
Henceforth, I shall honor Thee and obey Thy every word!
Praise be Christ Jesus, our Lord and Savior. Amen.

Lost in Despair

Lord, oh Lord, I need Your help now more than ever before.

What hope I had has gone out the door.

My book of prayer is on the shelf alone, amidst the dust of life and much folklore.

My life is filled with tears and despair. . .I have nowhere to go, nor people to help.

It is only You, oh Lord, that can help me now.

Please hear my plea and acknowledge my bow!

Answer my prayer and give me hope for a better life, here and now.

Through Christ Jesus, our Lord and Savior. Amen.

With Fear my Heart is Filled

When I was young and foolish, danger was never near!
I danced and laughed the days away, without a bit of fear.
But now that the sun is setting, the laughter has come and gone.
Life has slipped away, and the nights have gotten long!
In prayer, I hope to seek relief for all my wrongs. . .
And return to the days of happy music and light-hearted songs!
Dear Lord, please help me, my days are not long, not long!
All praise and glory be Yours on high, Lord Jesus, my Savior.
    Amen.

Peace

A Day of Wonder and Delight

The sun has set, and the hour has come.
The Lord has told me, my day is done.
As night approaches, I must thank Him on high,
For another day's work beneath a beautiful sky.
Thank you, oh Lord, for all you have done,
I must rest now until the return of the sun!
No more work and the end of fun . . .
Praise be Christ Jesus, our Lord and Savior. Amen.

The Bells

Church bells everywhere, dinging and ringing,
The city was rocking with sound, all around!
Not knowing what it was, I asked my Mom.
"The War is over," she said. "Your Dad is done!
His days are over, pounding the ground."
We can play again in the backyard on the giant swing!
It'll be like old times, not missing a thing.
The Big One, WWII, is done and over!
It's time to rejoice and roll in the clover!
Blessed by God forevermore.
With His most loving grace, we've won the race. Amen.

The Open Sea

As I gaze from the water's edge and look out toward eternity,
I cannot help but praise the Lord for sharing such beauty.
The calm waves bring us peace and a touch of happiness.
As they gently make their way to shore and never, never miss.
The fish within bring us food and nourishment, day after day.
As if the Lord himself ordered them to be calm and stay!
It is with praise and thanksgiving, I end this holyday.
Praise the Lord Jesus for another great day and a calm, peaceful
    night.
Amen.

The Wind

As I walk through the woods this beautiful morn, I am totally
free of doubt and scorn.

The swaying leaves and gentle sound bring back the early days,
before I became forlorn.

In the darkness of the woods, I find the deepest peace of mind.

I can leave my failure, anger and ill thoughts all behind.

Today is a new day, a new creation, a new gift from on-high.

As I finish my walk, I'm at peace again, knowing one day that I
shall finally join

Thee, beyond the sky!

Bless me, Lord Jesus, day-in and day-out, until we meet again!
Amen.

Progress

Acceptance

What I have found out this day of all days is that I am not really
in total control.

Whatever I do, however I finish, I have learned I need to accept
deep within my soul.

Thank you, Lord, for teaching me this great lesson, once again.

I have reviewed my work over and over, but it is not yet perfect,
so I shall cast it in the bin!

With new-found bliss and a rested mind, I will begin anew to
address my thoughts.

I will put pen to paper and think more deeply before I ink and
not be caught.

My work will be better, just wait and see. I'll accept from Thee
and enjoy my afternoon tea!

Bless the Lord Jesus on High. . .Thy kingdom come. Thy will be
done! Amen.

A Lesson Learned

Jesus, I wish I had your strength. I wish I had your trust.
In the heat of the night, I lose my thought and always claim I'm
    right!
But the following day, I quickly find my claim is just a bust!
With the Heavenly Father overhead, I need to act with faith,
honesty, and respect.
They will keep me honest, and close to Thee.
For it is in believing, I find faith, hope, and charity.
I need to follow what our heavenly Father suggests, 'Let it be, Let
    it be.'
In the name of Jesus Christ, our Savior and Victor. Amen.

A Slow Burn

Oh, Lord, you have given me eyes to see and faith to believe.

I am trying, oh Lord, I am trying hard, but within my soul, it is a
slow burn.

I know You are true, forgiving, and faithful, but I am very slow to
learn.

You are so high above the sky. All I can do is look up and sigh!

Forgive me, oh Lord, forgive me and purge my sins before I die.

'Tis time to come clean to one and all and expose my wrongs and
lies.

With your good grace and blessings, I can stoke the fire and end
up in heaven even higher!

Lord of hosts, have mercy on my soul. Show me the truth and
the way home to Thee.

Amen.

Seasons

Evening Prayer

As the twilight slowly fades and the day becomes night,
It is time to 'Praise the Lord' for another great day.
He has given us light and shown us the way. . .
Although darkness will shroud us, we will be alright.
We can praise God and have a peaceful rest tonight.
With his 'loving grace' he has given us so much,
Peace, Happiness, Joy, and eternal life, within sight.
Thank you, Lord. Oh, thank you so much. Your kindness
and grace will see us through to the end! Thank you and Amen.

Rise Up, My Son, Rise Up

Oh, Lord, forgive me, I've fallen again, physically, mentally, and
  spiritually.
Through your help and grace, I'll be able to mend, to change and
  recover
completely!
Forgive me my sins, I beg of Thee. I promise to change and mend
  my life.
I've had to deal with illness, poverty and unending strife. . .
But with Your help I can rise up again, to fight the good fight to
  the end of life.
I know I've said this once before, but I beg for forgiveness
  forevermore.
I need your grace now more than ever before.
Help me stand up straight and tall, and I shall spread faith to one
  and all.
In the name of Jesus Christ, my Savior. Amen.

Rising of the Sun

The stars have said 'good night' today, yet the moon wants to stay!
It's a tiny sliver in the heavens above, as the 'Boldest of Bold'
begins to shed its rays.
A small red streak crosses the horizon and pierces the morning
dew.
It's time to get up, dress in Fall working clothes, and let the coffee
brew.
The tractor is ready for a day's hard work, reaping and cutting
everything in sight.
Soon, that bold sun will show us the way to go straight ahead, left
or right.
Thank you, oh Lord, for all Your might, for letting us share
morning and night.
Without Your helping hand and plentiful grace, we'd not be able
to do what's right!
Amen.

Time to Plant

Oh, Lord, you've been so kind and dear.

Given us good health and fertile ground so near.

'Tis time to plant and share the crops in early Fall.

As you, Son of God, once did for sinners, saints, and all.

With your loving hands, you have given us this land, the good
and the ruins.

To enjoy, to share, to improve, groom and bloom!

Yet, we must keep our sites heavenly bound,

For the final call shall soon come from on high, not the soiled
ground!

Praises to thee, Lord Jesus, for your goodness and giving of self.

Without you, there would be nothing to share, nor happiness
near. Amen.

Thanks

Friends Around the World

Whether friends in the U.S., Europe, or the Far East,
You're all truly welcome to our humble feast.
We want you to know that distance is not a barrier.
We will find a way somehow, somewhere, to get the right carrier.
Blessings from the highest mountain peaks to all,
From the Rockies to the islands in the Bay of Bengal.
Thank you, Lord, for our many friends, wherever they may be.
    Amen.

Love of Life

As I walk down the path today, I think I have found the gift at
last, the gift of life.

I need not worry, and can cast away all prior thoughts and strife.

The Lord's welcoming arms will open to see me soon.

But I have time to share this gift and give praise before the final
noon.

I must hurry now and share with others the joy I have found.

I have a mission, a direction, and a purpose, so I can no longer
lounge!

All praise to God overhead with arms extended, open to all,

as he has forever intended. Amen.

Oh Lord, I Thank Thee for My Loved One!

Through many years and tears, we have walked together,
Shared our thoughts and raised a family too, even better!
There were some moments of doubt and stress,
But with Your help, we have made it through, nonetheless.
Thank you, Lord. Thank you, Lord, for all the rest.
Thanks to Christ Jesus, our Lord and Savior. Amen.

The Touch of Spring

With high praise, comforting winds, and a smiling grin,
I walk the walk, while praising the Lord once again!
He has shown his kindness and shared with Mother Earth.
She has shown her thanks and bounced back from winter with all
    she is worth!
The tulips are up, the trees are budding, and other flowers will
    soon follow.
Even the birds have returned and searched for new spring
    hollows.
All this the Lord has given and more. . .
In the face of such beauty and love, it makes one feel like a
    newborn dove!
Wonderful, Jesus, I thank Thee for your wonders and kindness,
To bless our land with flowers and growth. Amen.

www.ingramcontent.com/pod-product-compliance
Lightning Source LLC
Chambersburg PA
CBHW050603280326
41933CB00011B/1960